CATS SET V
The Designer Cats

TOYGER CATS

Jill C. Wheeler
ABDO Publishing Company

visit us at
www.abdopublishing.com

Published by ABDO Publishing Company, 8000 West 78th Street, Edina, Minnesota 55439. Copyright © 2011 by Abdo Consulting Group, Inc. International copyrights reserved in all countries. No part of this book may be reproduced in any form without written permission from the publisher. The Checkerboard Library™ is a trademark and logo of ABDO Publishing Company.

Printed in the United States of America, North Mankato, Minnesota.
092010
012011

 PRINTED ON RECYCLED PAPER

Cover Photo: Photo by Helmi Flick
Interior Photos: Photo by Helmi Flick pp. 5, 9, 11, 13, 15, 17, 19, 21; Photolibrary p. 7

Series Coordinator: Heidi M.D. Elston
Editors: Heidi M.D. Elston, BreAnn Rumsch
Cover & Interior Design: Neil Klinepier
Production Layout: Jaime Martens

Library of Congress Cataloging-in-Publication Data

Wheeler, Jill C., 1964-
  Toyger cats / Jill C. Wheeler.
     p. cm. -- (Cats. Set V, Designer cats)
  Includes bibliographical references and index.
  ISBN 978-1-60453-733-8 (alk. paper)
  1. Toyger cat--Juvenile literature. I. Title.
  SF449.T69W44 2010
  636.8--dc22
                                        2009021146

Thinking about a Designer Cat?
Some communities have laws that regulate hybrid animal ownership. Be sure to check with your local authorities before buying a hybrid kitten.

CONTENTS

A New Call of the Wild

First there were tigers. Now there are toygers. Yet, these **exotic**-looking cats are not found in forests and tall grasses. Instead, toygers roam the homes of many cat lovers.

Toygers are among the newest designer cats. Designer cats are **bred** to look like a wildcat. But, breeders hope they will have the lovable personality of a domestic, or tame, cat.

The toyger is bred to look like a small version of the Asian tiger. However, the toyger has no tiger blood. It is a cross between a domestic shorthair tabby cat and a Bengal cat.

Domestic cats are affectionate and easy to care for. In addition, their small size makes them a good fit for houses and apartments.

Like all cats, toygers are members of the family **Felidae**. This family has 37 different species. These include the big wildcats such as lions, panthers, and tigers.

TIGERS

The tiger is the largest member of the family **Felidae**. Wild tigers are found only in Asia. They can grow up to 13 feet (4 m) long. And, they may weigh more than 600 pounds (270 kg)!

These huge cats are beautiful creatures. They range in color from brownish yellow to orange red. Their coats are marked by black stripes. Each tiger's stripe pattern is one of a kind. It is as distinctive as a human fingerprint.

Tigers used to be widespread in Asia. However, their numbers have dropped because of illegal hunting and loss of **habitat**. Three of the nine tiger **subspecies** are now extinct. Today, there are only about 4,000 tigers left in the wild.

Toyger founder Judy Sugden hopes the toyger will inspire people to help protect wild tigers.

DOMESTIC CATS

To create a toyger, **breeders** cross a domestic shorthair tabby and a Bengal cat. These two cats help give the toyger just the right tiger look.

The striped coat of a domestic shorthair tabby is similar to a tiger's coat. In addition, domestic shorthairs are known for their friendly personalities. They get along well with children and dogs. This makes them ideal family pets.

The Bengal cat was chosen for toyger breeding because of its body type. Bengals also display an **exotic**-looking coat. This domestic cat is a **hybrid**. One of its parents is a wildcat called the Asian leopard cat. The other parent is a domestic breed of cat.

Left:
A mackerel tabby domestic shorthair

Below:
The Bengal cat was developed by breeder Jean Mill. She is toyger creator Judy Sugden's mother.

THE BEGINNING

Judy Sugden **bred** the first toyger in the 1980s. She hoped to create a domestic cat that looked like a tiger.

One major obstacle Sugden faced was imitating the tiger's facial markings. A tiger has circular markings on the head. A domestic cat generally doesn't have patterns around the temples. And, the stripes on the head are usually vertical.

Then in 1993, Sugden found a male street cat in Kashmir, India. He had spots on the top of his head. Sugden hoped to create a tiger pattern from these markings.

Sugden bred her male street cat with some of her earlier toygers. Eventually, the kittens displayed stripes around their temples.

The toyger **hybrid** is still a work in progress. Each generation comes one step closer to matching the striking look of the tiger.

Appearance is very important to toyger breeders.

TOYGER CATS

Toygers are beautiful **hybrid** animals. They look like tiny versions of the tigers seen in zoos or on television. They move similarly to wild tigers, too. Toygers are powerful yet graceful.

The toyger is a medium-sized cat with short hair. It has an athletic build, with good bone structure and muscle tone.

This domestic cat's ears are small and rounded. Its eyes are set wide apart. They are medium in size and almond shaped. The toyger can have long toes and large feet. It carries its long tail low.

Breeders continue to develop the toyger. They hope it will one day have shorter ears and smaller eyes. And, they want it to have a wider nose tip and a bigger chin. That way, the toyger will look even more like a tiger.

Toygers get many of their features from the Bengal cat.

BEHAVIOR

Toygers make great pets. Some owners compare their toygers to dogs. Toygers are dependable, affectionate, and gentle. They can even learn to walk on a leash. These **hybrid** cats can also be very alert and athletic. They like active play with toys and people.

Toygers are family friendly, too. Their size and personality make them suitable for most households. Toygers enjoy being around people, including children. They also get along well with other pets.

Unlike most domestic cats, toygers enjoy playing in water. This makes them much like their wild tiger cousins. Tigers are strong swimmers and enjoy bathing.

Toygers are active, energetic cats. They need room to run and pounce.

Coats & Colors

The toyger's coloring and markings set it apart from other domestic cats. These features have helped make it what some call America's next superpet.

The toyger coat is short with thick, luxurious, soft fur. It must also be glittery. The ideal toyger coat is a bright pumpkin color with very dark stripes. Like a tiger, the stripes should be bold and nonuniform.

The toyger's throat, chin, and cheeks should be white. White fur should also surround the eyes and the lower whiskers. This coloring should sweep upward onto the temples and the forehead. The paw pads and the tip of the tail must be black.

The orange color of most toyger kittens deepens as they age.

SIZES

Tigers are the largest of all cats. Yet, this does not mean toygers are big pets. In fact, they are only slightly larger than most common house cats.

Male toygers usually weigh more than females. When fully grown, males range from 15 to 17 pounds (7 to 8 kg). Females weigh between 7 and 10 pounds (3 and 5 kg).

In comparison, the average domestic cat weighs between 6 and 10 pounds (3 and 5 kg). Yet, its bone structure and long tail may make it appear larger.

Most newborn kittens weigh just 3.5 ounces (99 g). They cannot see or hear. So, they depend on their mother for care.

A toyger must give
the impression of
a tiger.

CARE

One reason domestic cats make great pets is that they are easy to care for. That is true of toygers as well. Like many house cats, toygers can learn to use a **litter box**.

Toygers usually do not require special food. A high-quality cat food and fresh water will help keep this **hybrid** happy.

Toygers are generally very healthy. Still, a veterinarian can help care for a toyger. Like all domestic cats, toygers need **vaccines**. And if they are not being **bred**, they should be **spayed** or **neutered**.

Females that do become **pregnant** carry their young for about nine weeks. On average, they may have three to five kittens.

Owners need to set aside time to play with their toygers.

Owners can expect a toyger to live for 10 to 15 years. This is similar to many domestic cats. With proper care, a toyger will be a welcome addition to any loving family.

GLOSSARY

breed - a group of animals sharing the same ancestors and appearance. A breeder is a person who raises animals. Raising animals is often called breeding them.

exotic - strikingly, excitingly, or mysteriously different or unusual.

Felidae (FEHL-uh-dee) - the scientific Latin name for the cat family. Members of this family are called felids. They include domestic cats, lions, tigers, leopards, jaguars, cougars, wildcats, lynx, and cheetahs.

habitat - a place where a living thing is naturally found.

hybrid - an offspring of two animals or plants of different races, breeds, varieties, species, or genera.

litter box - a box filled with cat litter, which is similar to sand. Cats use litter boxes to dispose of their waste.

neuter (NOO-tuhr) - to remove a male animal's reproductive organs.

pregnant - having one or more babies growing within the body.

spay - to remove a female animal's reproductive organs.

subspecies - a group of related organisms ranking below a species. Members of a subspecies often share a common geographic range.

vaccine (vak-SEEN) - a shot given to animals or humans to prevent them from getting an illness or a disease.

WEB SITES

To learn more about toyger cats, visit ABDO Publishing Company online. Web sites about toyger cats are featured on our Book Links page. These links are routinely monitored and updated to provide the most current information available.

www.abdopublishing.com

INDEX